UNCHARTED: STORIES OF SURVIVAL

T0011174

TORNADO Terror!

by Harriet McGregor

Illustrations by Alan Brown

BEARPORT PUBLISHING

Minneapolis, Minnesota

BEAR CLAW

Credits: 21, © Minerva Studio/Shutterstock; 22, © James Kirkikis 22/Shutterstock; 23, © Christopher Slater/Shutterstock.

Supervising Editor: Allison Juda
Editor: Sarah Eason
Proofreader: Jennifer Sanderson
Designer: Paul Myerscough

DISCLAIMER: This graphic story is a dramatization based on true events. It is intended to give the reader a sense of the narrative rather than a presentation of actual details as they occurred.

Library of Congress Cataloging-in-Publication Data

Names: McGregor, Harriet, author. | Brown, Alan (Illustrator), illustrator.

Title: Tornado terror! / by Harriet McGregor ; illustrations by Alan Brown.

Description: Bear claw edition. | Minneapolis, Minnesota : Bearport Publishing, [2021] | Series: Uncharted: stories of survival | Includes bibliographical references and index.
Identifiers: LCCN 2020008647 (print) | LCCN 2020008648 (ebook) | ISBN 9781647470357 (library binding) | ISBN 9781647470425 (paperback) | ISBN 9781647470494 (ebook)
Subjects: LCSH: Tornadoes–Juvenile literature. | Tornadoes–Comic books, strips, etc. | Graphic novels.
Classification: LCC QC955.2 .M38 2021 (print) | LCC QC955.2 (ebook) | DDC 363.34/923–dc23
LC record available at https://lccn.loc.gov/2020008647
LC ebook record available at https://lccn.loc.gov/2020008648

For more information, write to Bearport Publishing, 5357 Penn Avenue South, Minneapolis, MN 55419. Printed in the United States of America.

CONTENTS

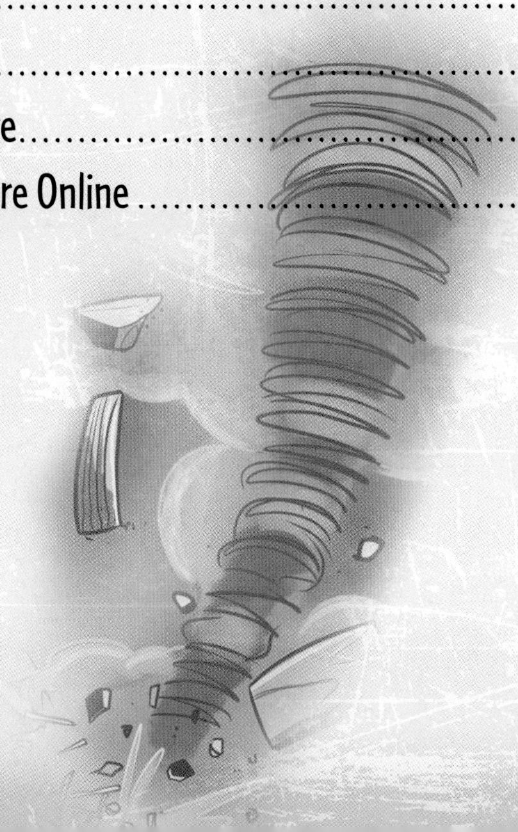

Chapter 1

REMEMBERING THE TORNADO

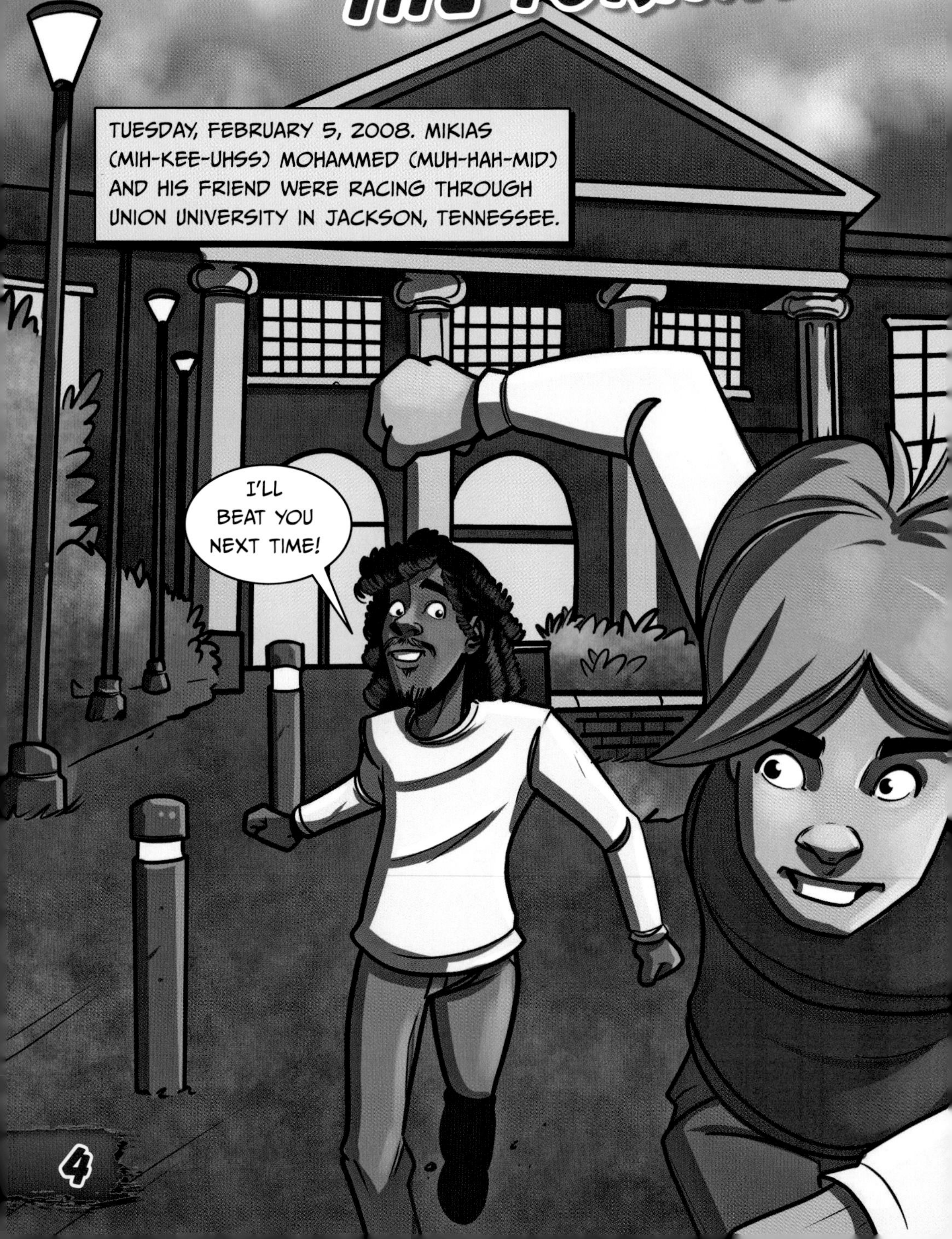
TUESDAY, FEBRUARY 5, 2008. MIKIAS (MIH-KEE-UHSS) MOHAMMED (MUH-HAH-MID) AND HIS FRIEND WERE RACING THROUGH UNION UNIVERSITY IN JACKSON, TENNESSEE.
I'LL BEAT YOU NEXT TIME!

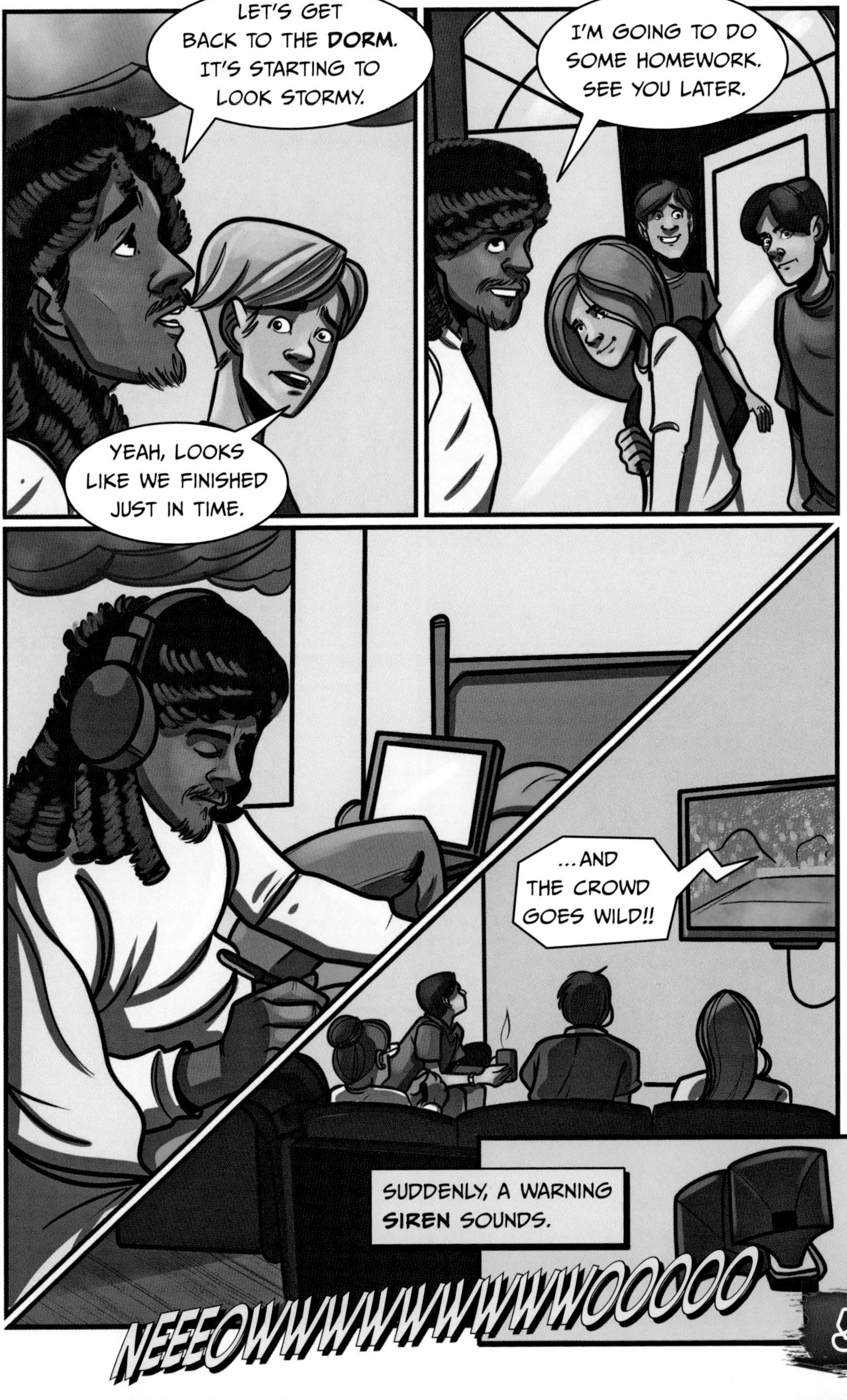
LET'S GET BACK TO THE **DORM.** IT'S STARTING TO LOOK STORMY.
YEAH, LOOKS LIKE WE FINISHED JUST IN TIME.
I'M GOING TO DO SOME HOMEWORK. SEE YOU LATER.
...AND THE CROWD GOES WILD!!
SUDDENLY, A WARNING **SIREN** SOUNDS.
NEEEOWWWWWWWWWWWOOOOOO

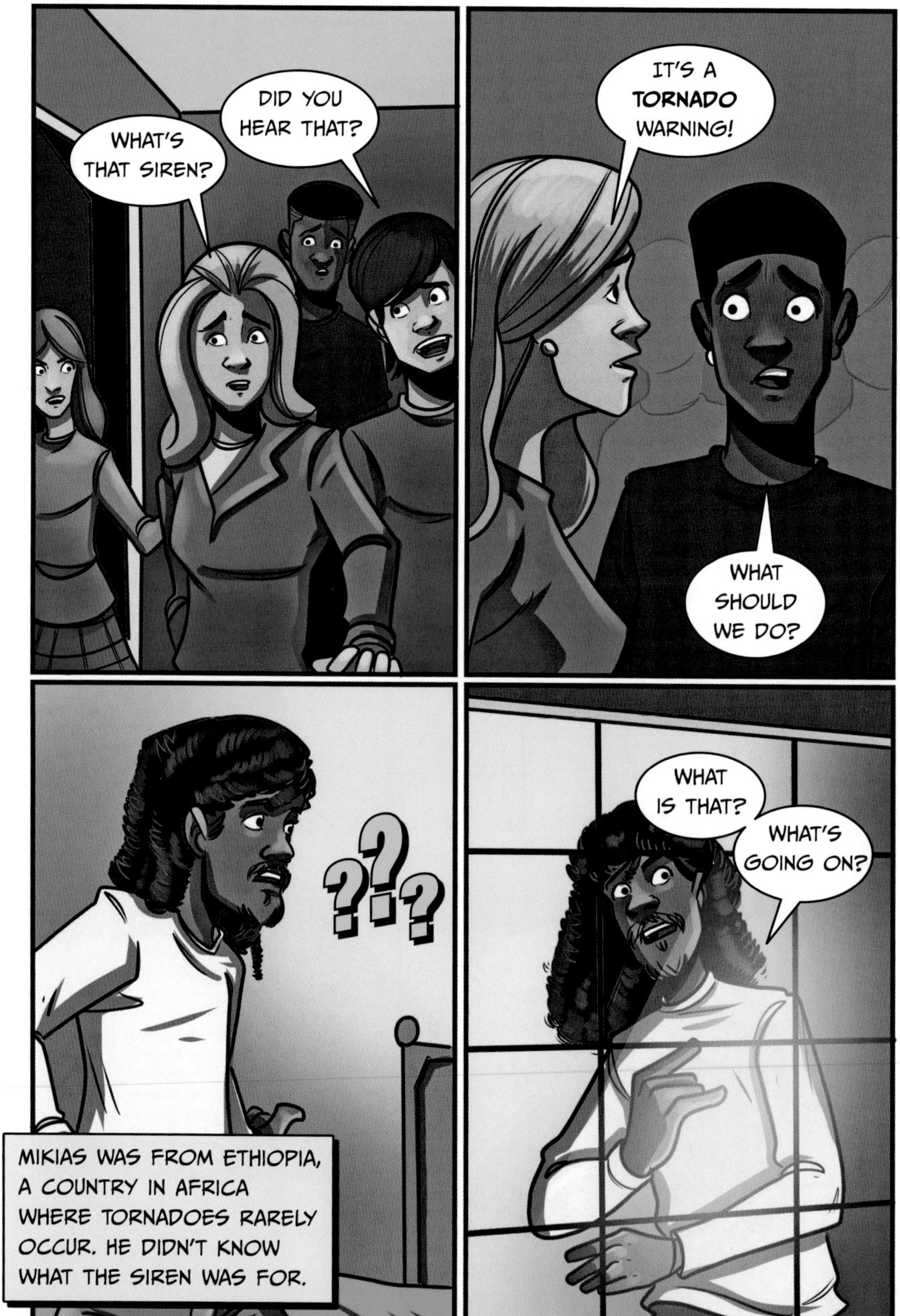
WHAT'S THAT SIREN?
DID YOU HEAR THAT?
IT'S A **TORNADO** WARNING!
WHAT SHOULD WE DO?
???
MIKIAS WAS FROM ETHIOPIA, A COUNTRY IN AFRICA WHERE TORNADOES RARELY OCCUR. HE DIDN'T KNOW WHAT THE SIREN WAS FOR.
WHAT IS THAT?
WHAT'S GOING ON?

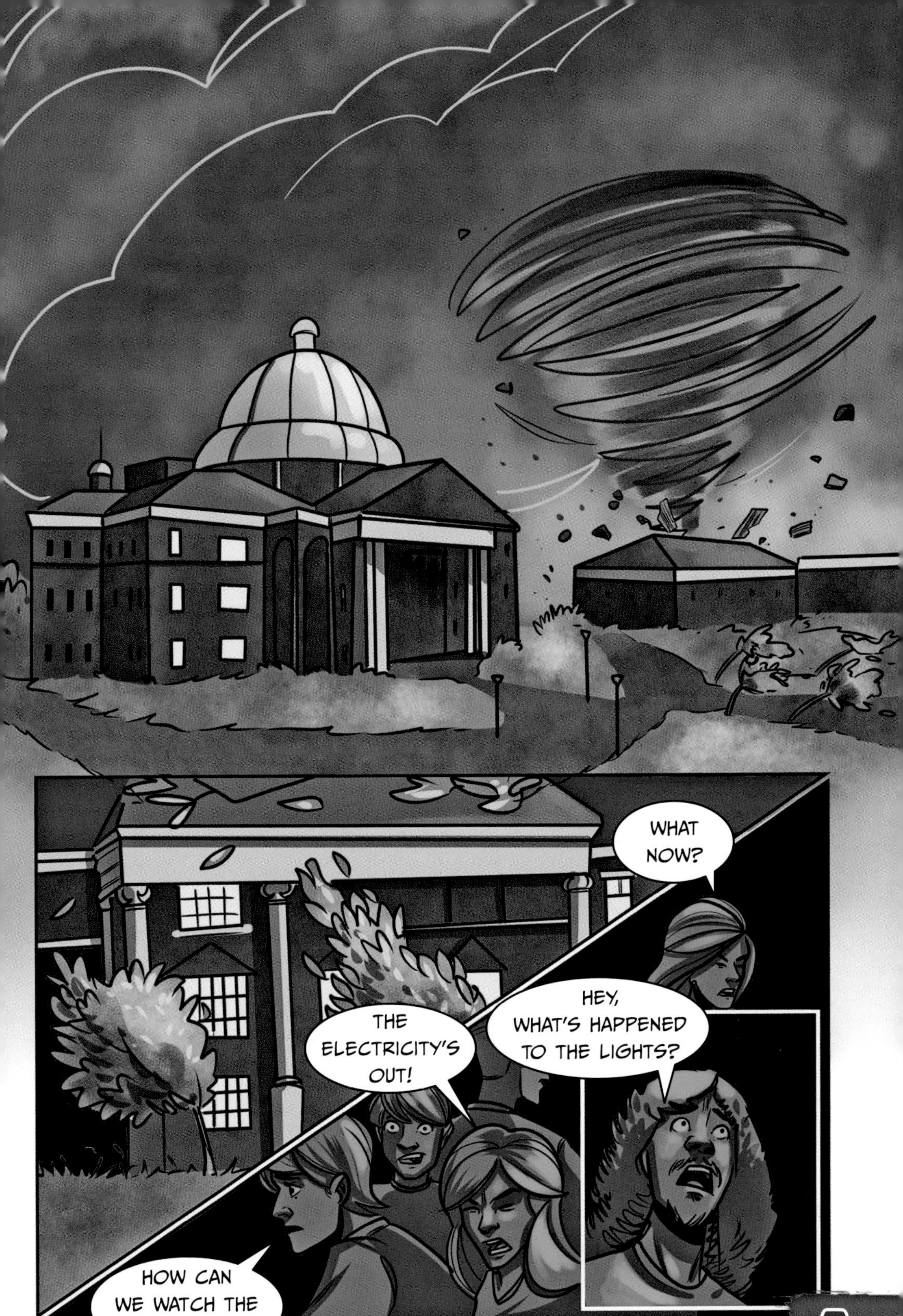
WHAT NOW?
HEY, WHAT'S HAPPENED TO THE LIGHTS?
THE ELECTRICITY'S OUT!
HOW CAN WE WATCH THE GAME NOW?

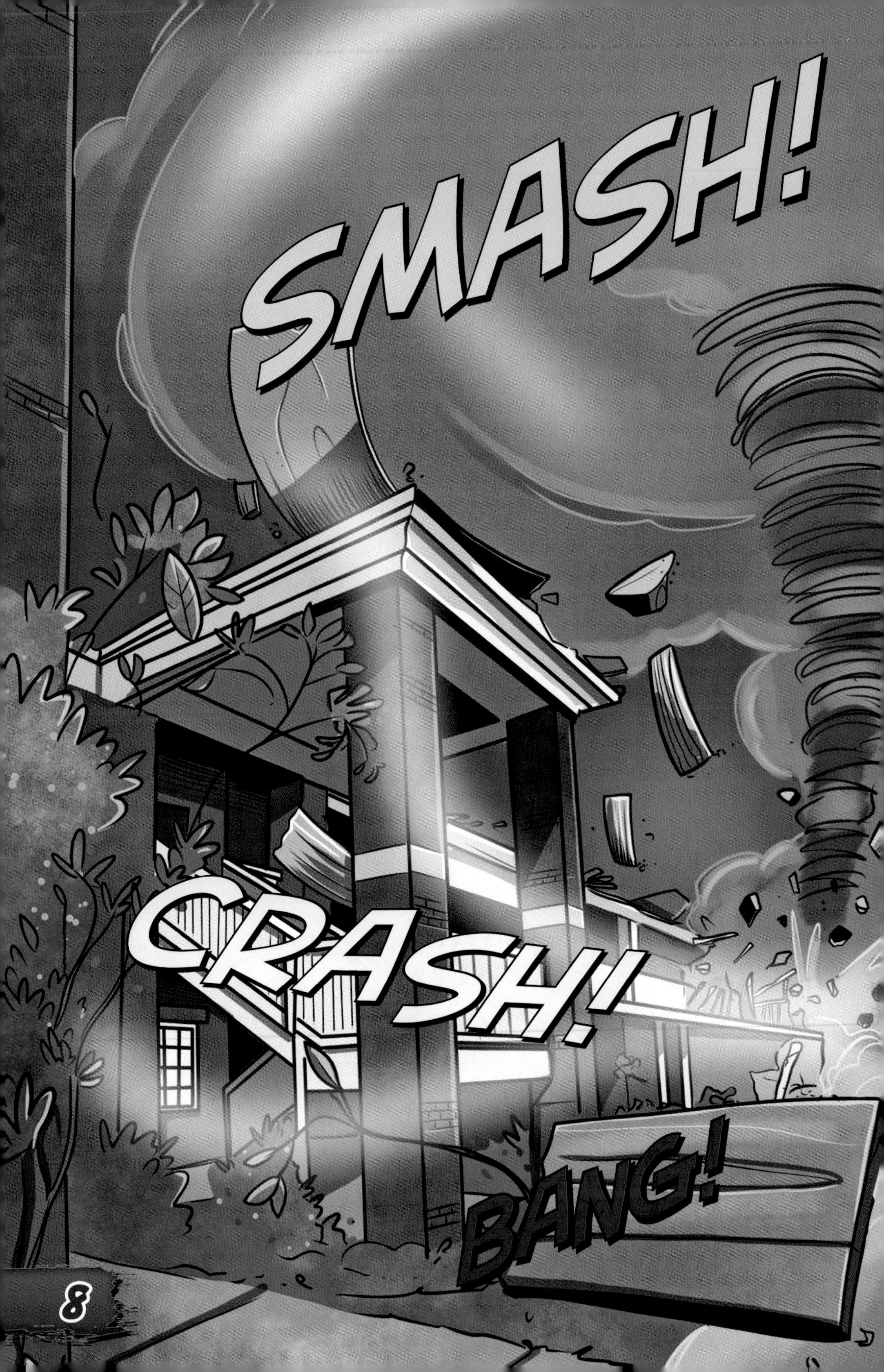
SMASH!
CRASH!
BANG!

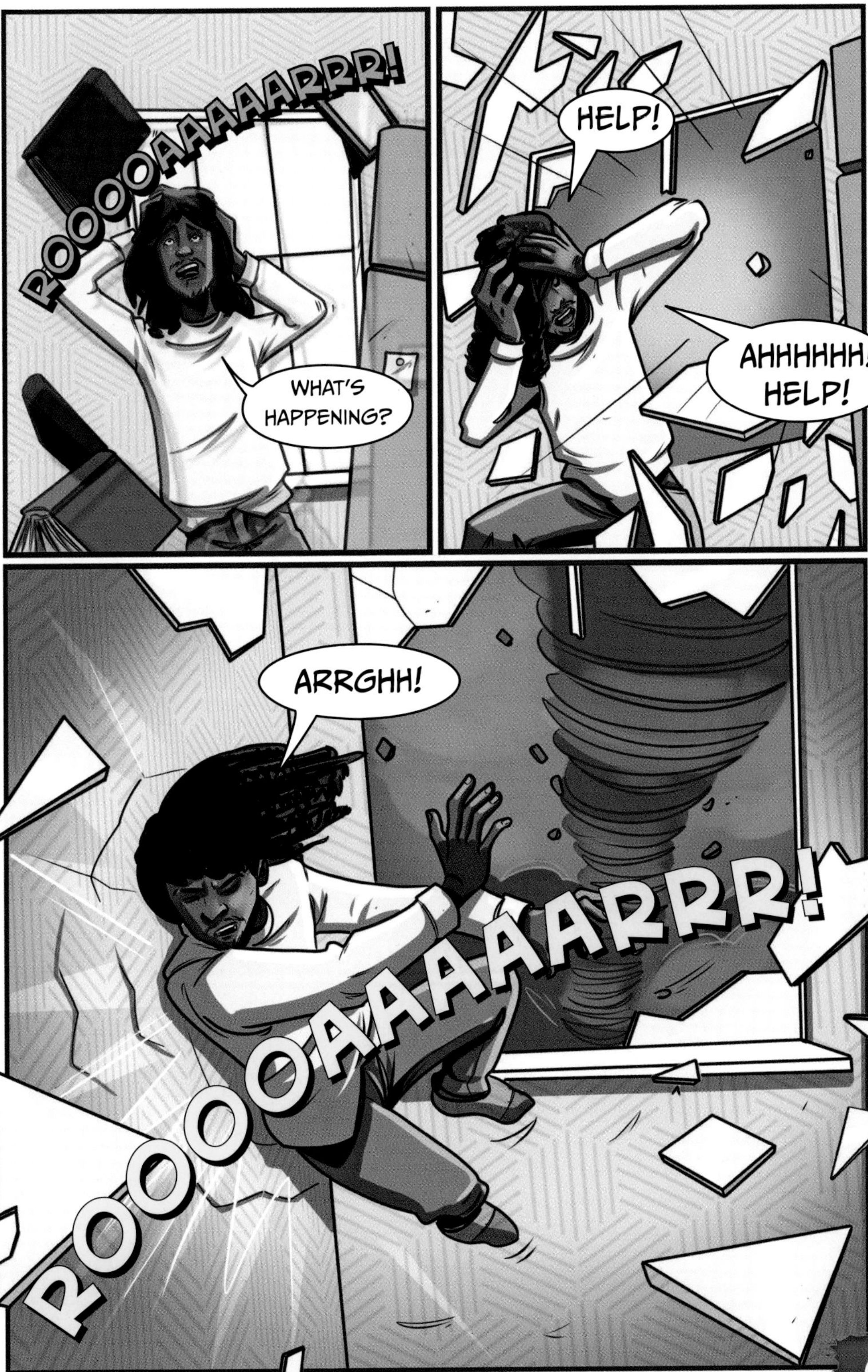
ROOOOAAAAARRR!
WHAT'S HAPPENING?
HELP!
AHHHHHH! HELP!
ARRGHH!
ROOOOAAAAARRR!

Chapter 2

SURVIVING THE TORNADO

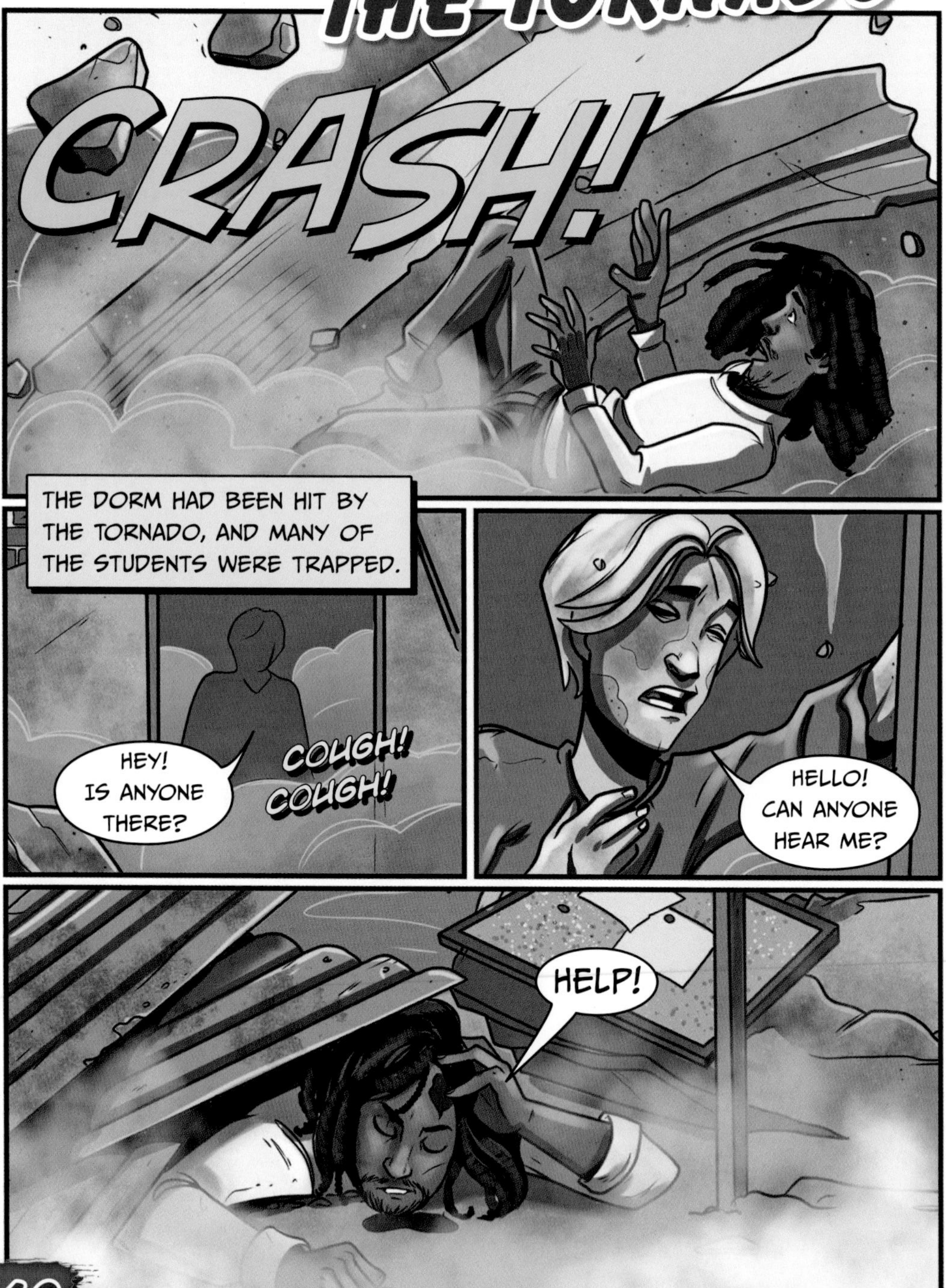
CRASH!
THE DORM HAD BEEN HIT BY THE TORNADO, AND MANY OF THE STUDENTS WERE TRAPPED.
HEY! IS ANYONE THERE?
COUGH! COUGH!
HELLO! CAN ANYONE HEAR ME?
HELP!

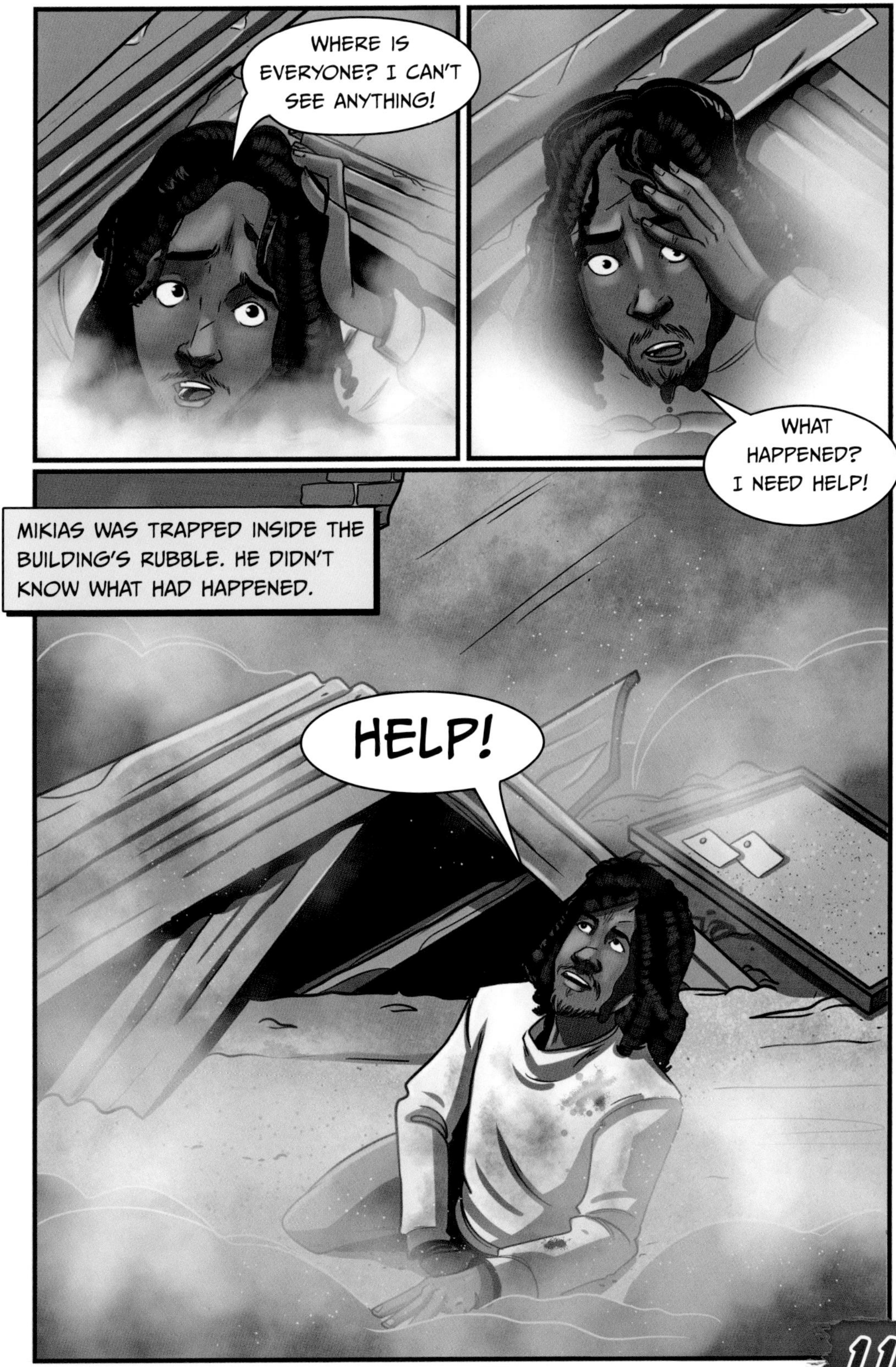
WHERE IS EVERYONE? I CAN'T SEE ANYTHING!
WHAT HAPPENED? I NEED HELP!
MIKIAS WAS TRAPPED INSIDE THE BUILDING'S RUBBLE. HE DIDN'T KNOW WHAT HAD HAPPENED.
HELP!

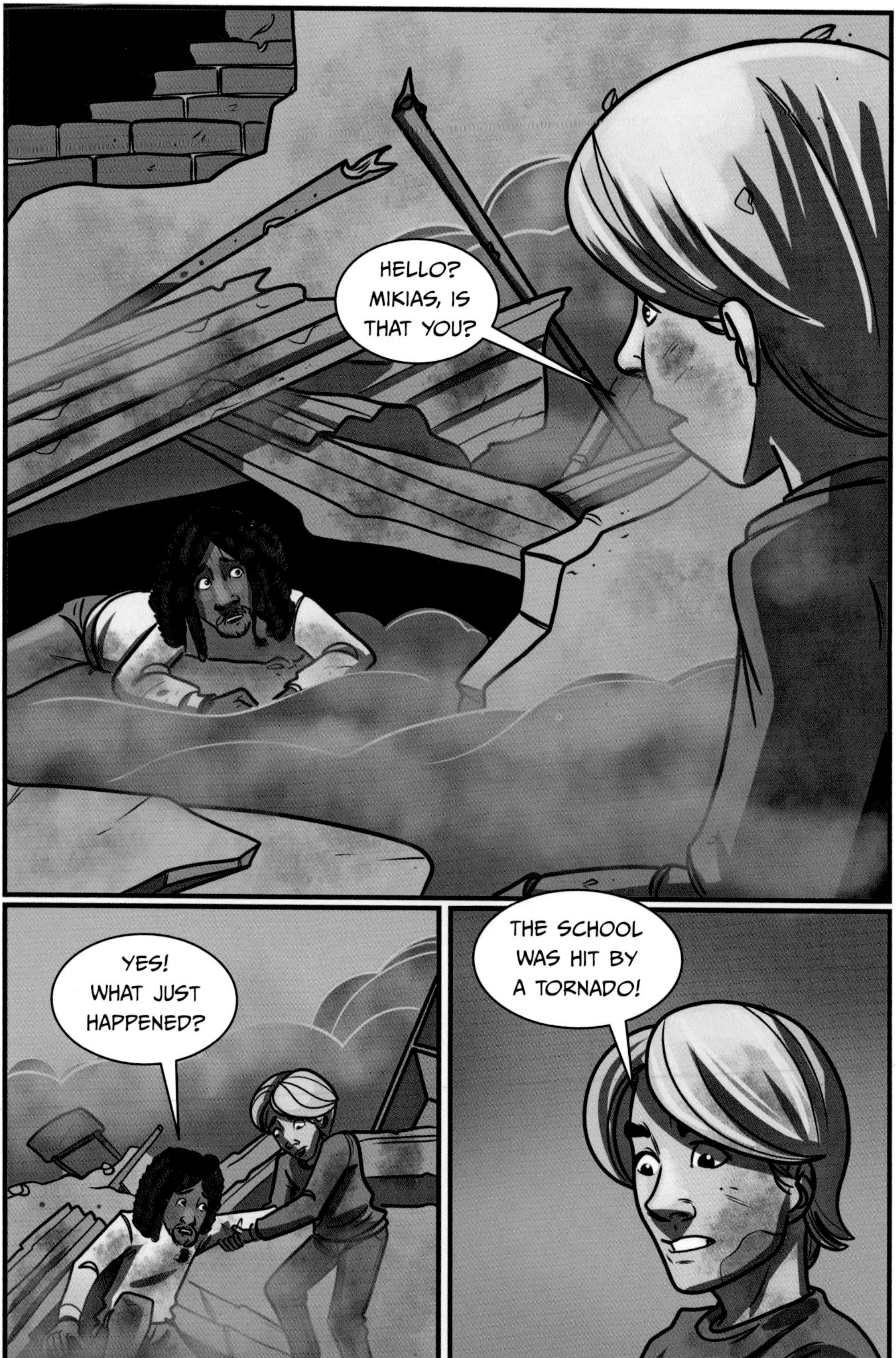
HELLO? MIKIAS, IS THAT YOU?
YES! WHAT JUST HAPPENED?
THE SCHOOL WAS HIT BY A TORNADO!

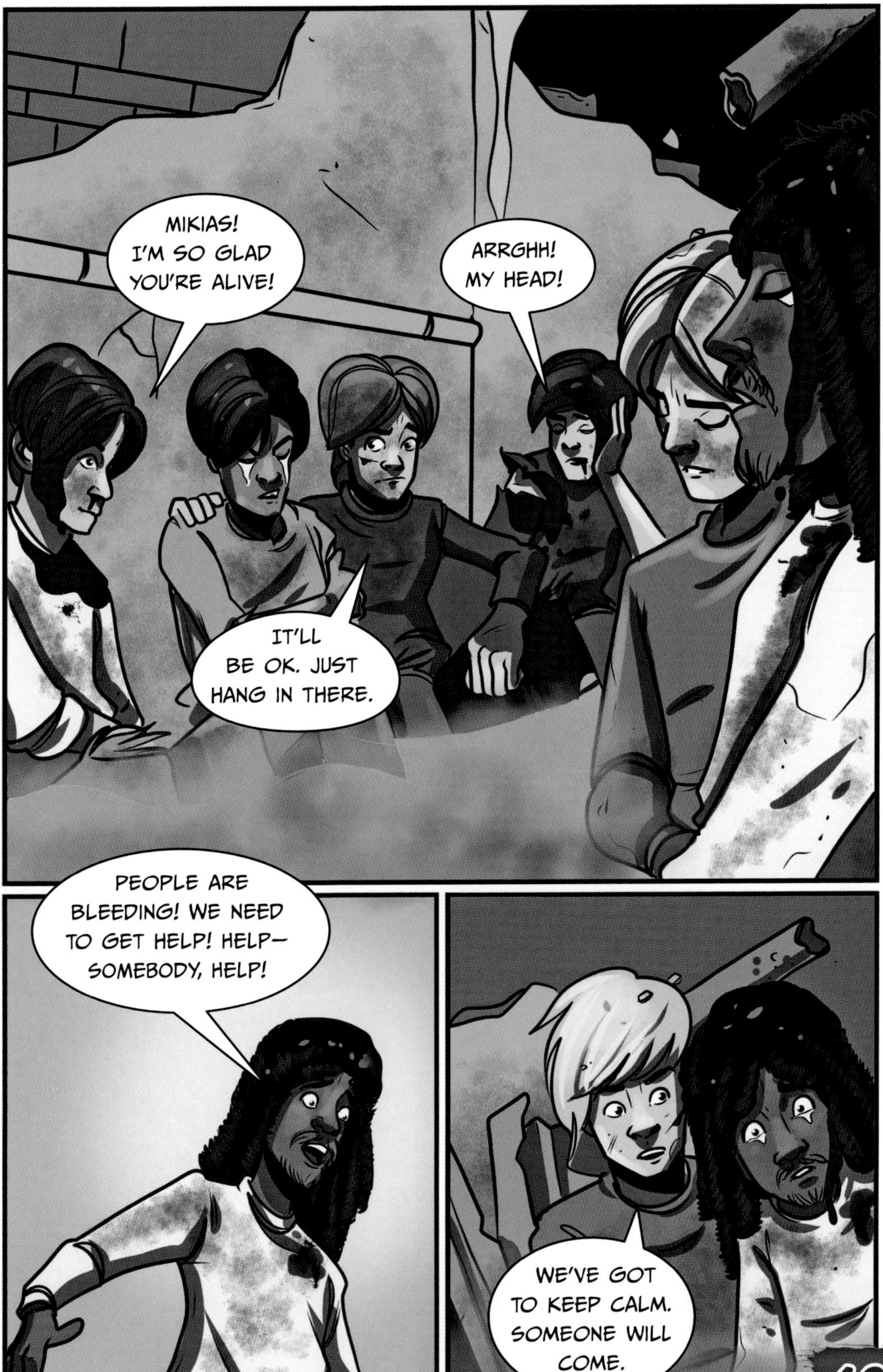
MIKIAS! I'M SO GLAD YOU'RE ALIVE!
ARRGHH! MY HEAD!
IT'LL BE OK. JUST HANG IN THERE.
PEOPLE ARE BLEEDING! WE NEED TO GET HELP! HELP— SOMEBODY, HELP!
WE'VE GOT TO KEEP CALM. SOMEONE WILL COME.

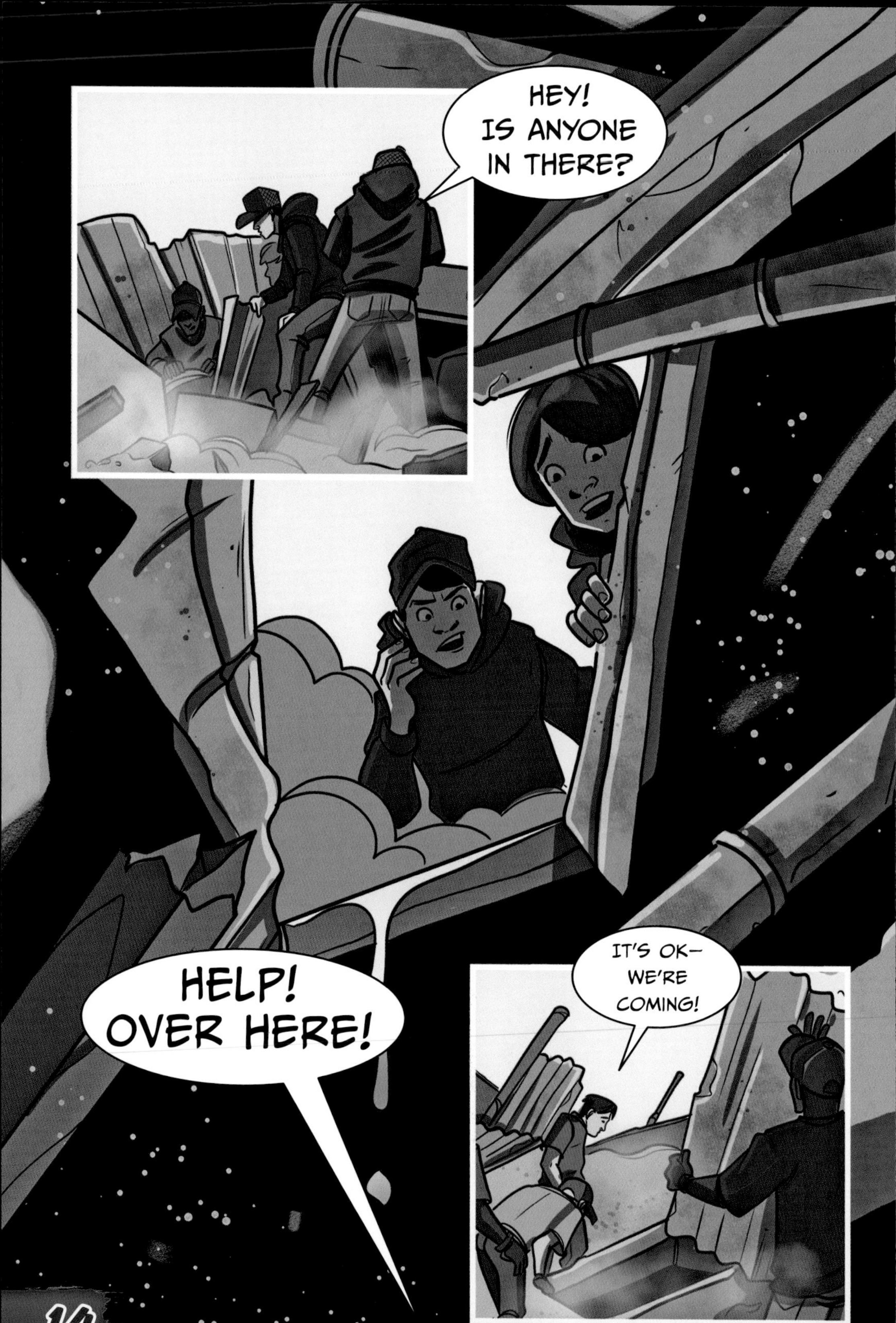
HEY! IS ANYONE IN THERE?
HELP! OVER HERE!
IT'S OK— WE'RE COMING!

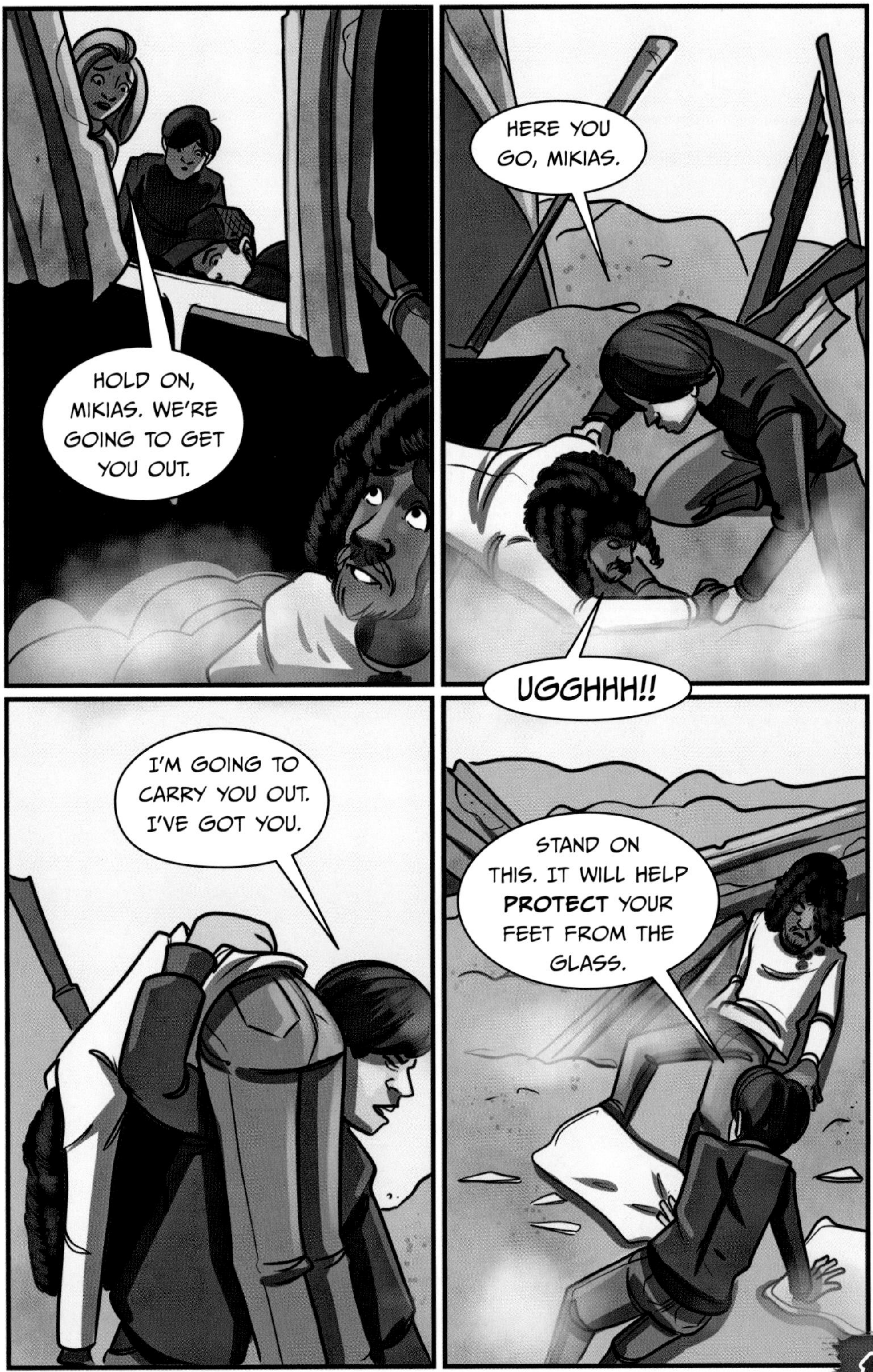
HOLD ON, MIKIAS. WE'RE GOING TO GET YOU OUT.
HERE YOU GO, MIKIAS.
UGGHHH!!
I'M GOING TO CARRY YOU OUT. I'VE GOT YOU.
STAND ON THIS. IT WILL HELP **PROTECT** YOUR FEET FROM THE GLASS.

Chapter 3

AFTER THE TORNADO

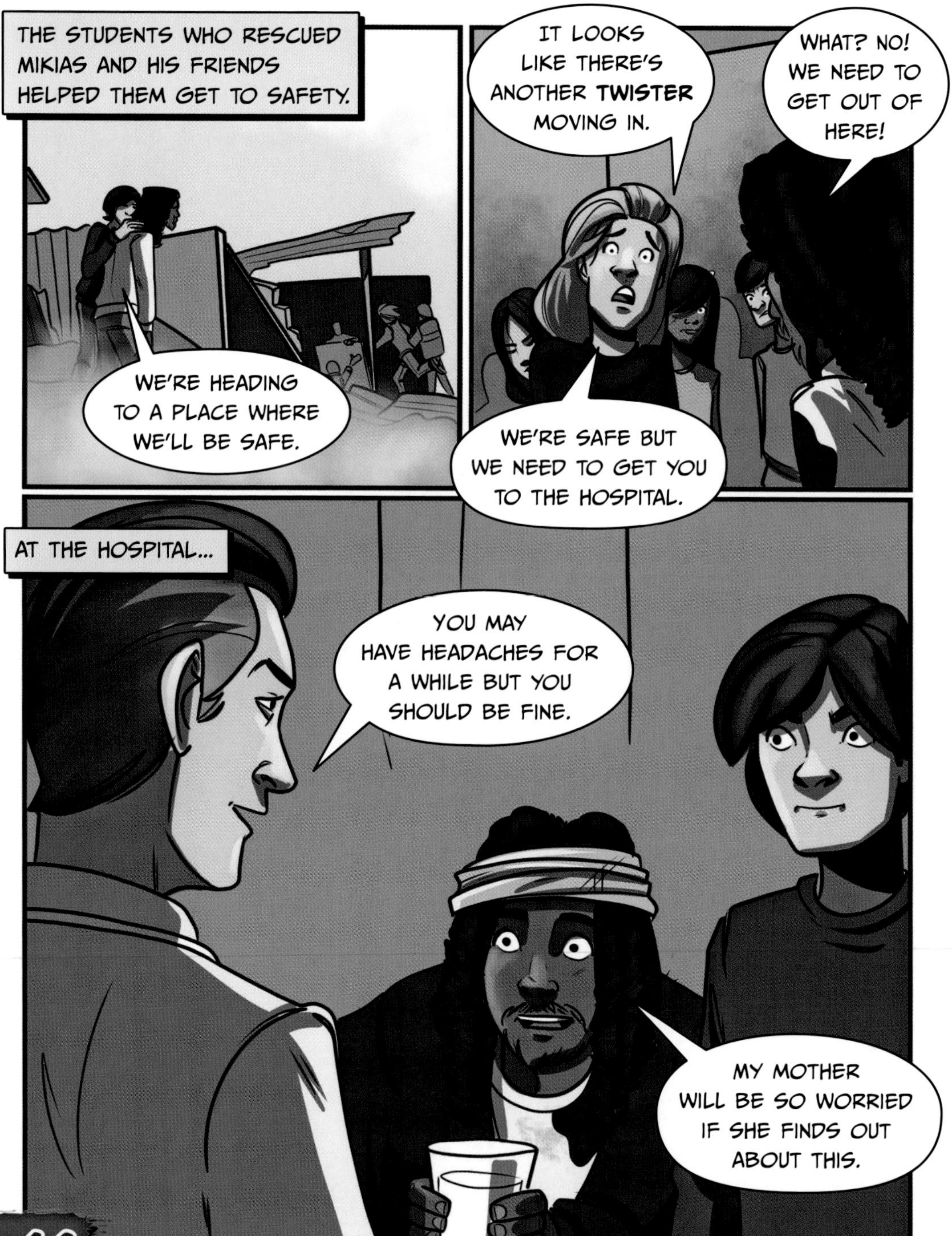
THE STUDENTS WHO RESCUED MIKIAS AND HIS FRIENDS HELPED THEM GET TO SAFETY.
WE'RE HEADING TO A PLACE WHERE WE'LL BE SAFE.
IT LOOKS LIKE THERE'S ANOTHER **TWISTER** MOVING IN.
WHAT? NO! WE NEED TO GET OUT OF HERE!
WE'RE SAFE BUT WE NEED TO GET YOU TO THE HOSPITAL.
AT THE HOSPITAL...
YOU MAY HAVE HEADACHES FOR A WHILE BUT YOU SHOULD BE FINE.
MY MOTHER WILL BE SO WORRIED IF SHE FINDS OUT ABOUT THIS.

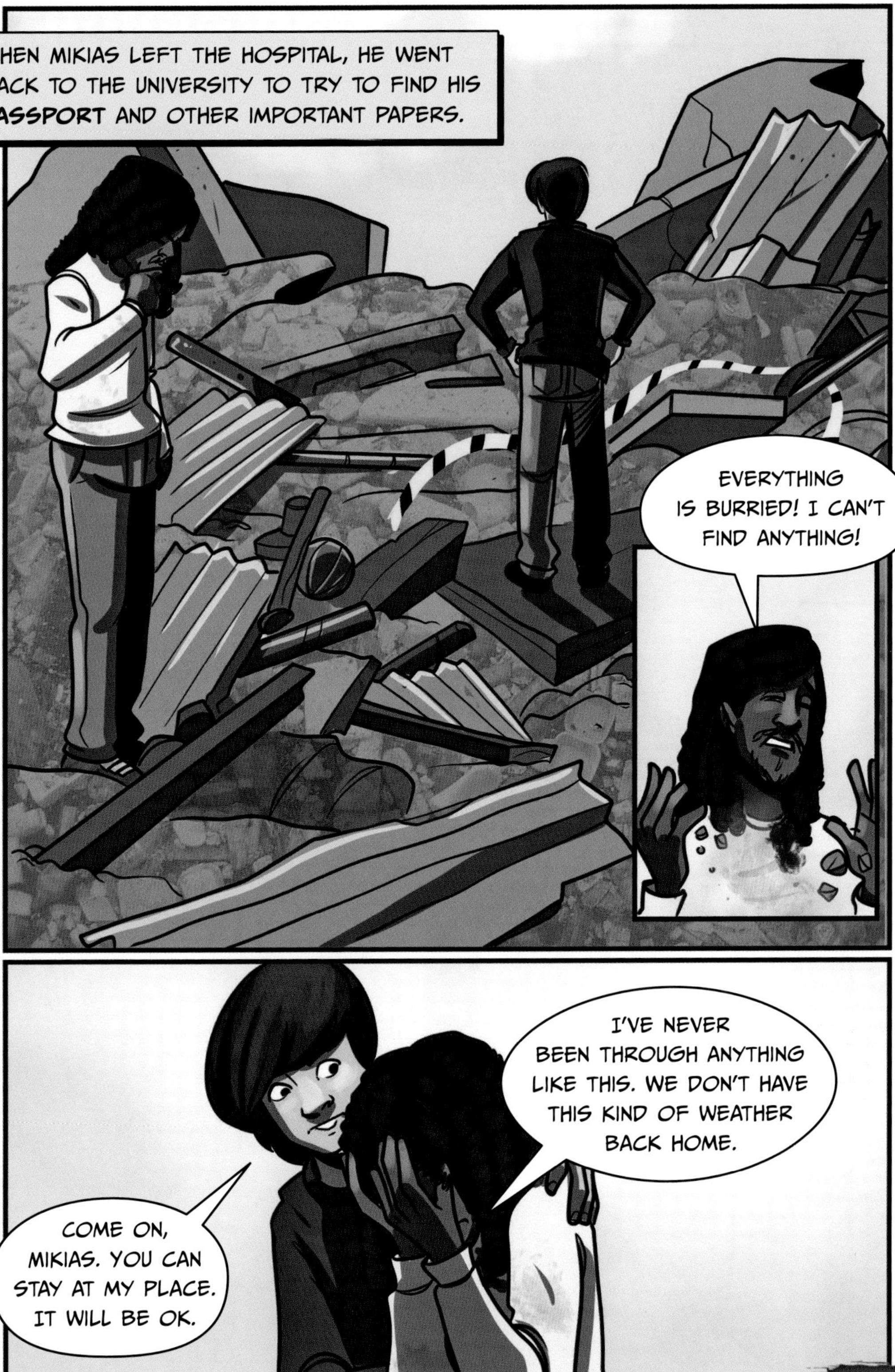
WHEN MIKIAS LEFT THE HOSPITAL, HE WENT BACK TO THE UNIVERSITY TO TRY TO FIND HIS **PASSPORT** AND OTHER IMPORTANT PAPERS.
EVERYTHING IS BURRIED! I CAN'T FIND ANYTHING!
I'VE NEVER BEEN THROUGH ANYTHING LIKE THIS. WE DON'T HAVE THIS KIND OF WEATHER BACK HOME.
COME ON, MIKIAS. YOU CAN STAY AT MY PLACE. IT WILL BE OK.

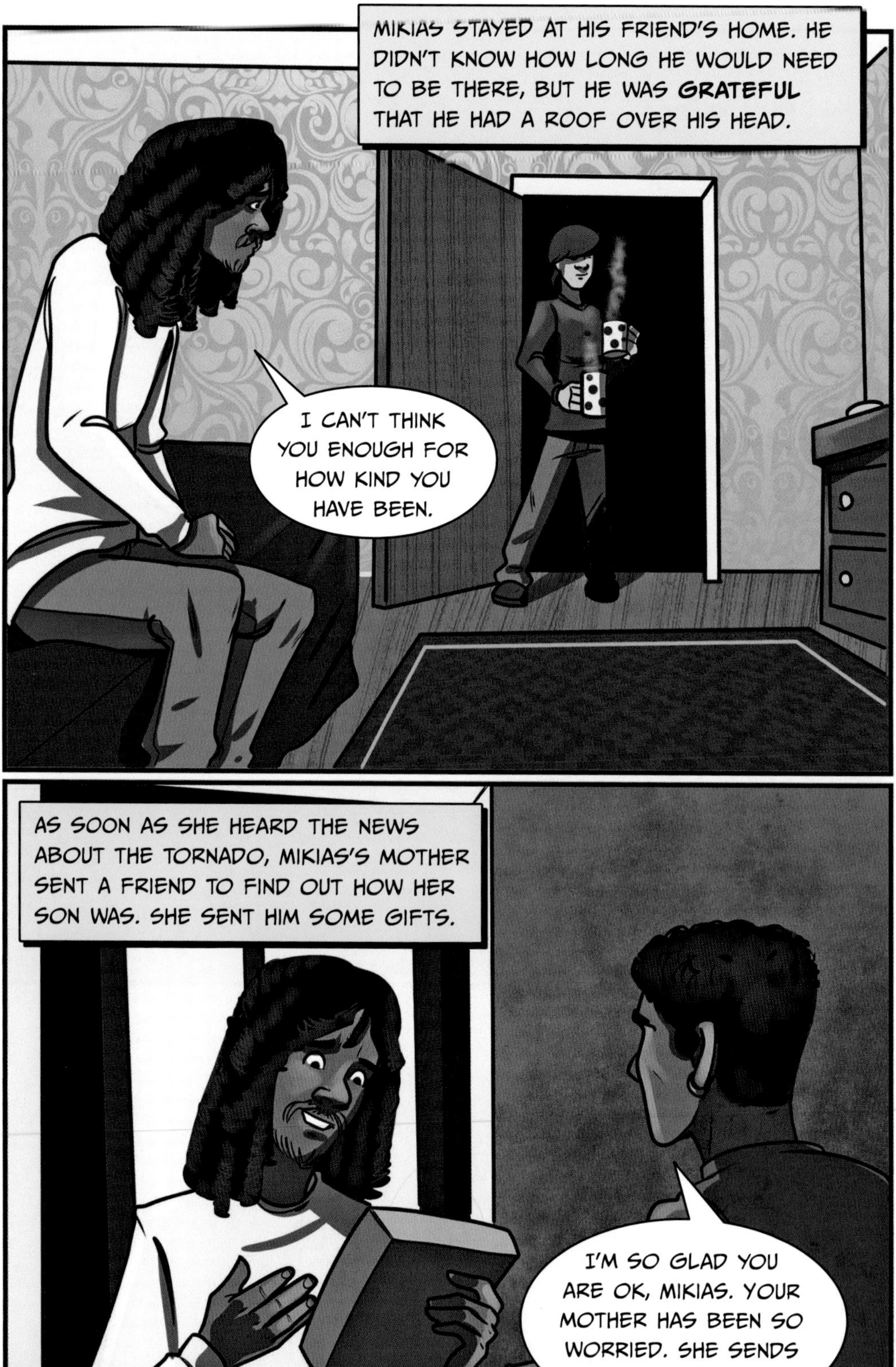
MIKIAS STAYED AT HIS FRIEND'S HOME. HE DIDN'T KNOW HOW LONG HE WOULD NEED TO BE THERE, BUT HE WAS **GRATEFUL** THAT HE HAD A ROOF OVER HIS HEAD.
I CAN'T THINK YOU ENOUGH FOR HOW KIND YOU HAVE BEEN.
AS SOON AS SHE HEARD THE NEWS ABOUT THE TORNADO, MIKIAS'S MOTHER SENT A FRIEND TO FIND OUT HOW HER SON WAS. SHE SENT HIM SOME GIFTS.
I'M SO GLAD YOU ARE OK, MIKIAS. YOUR MOTHER HAS BEEN SO WORRIED. SHE SENDS HER LOVE.

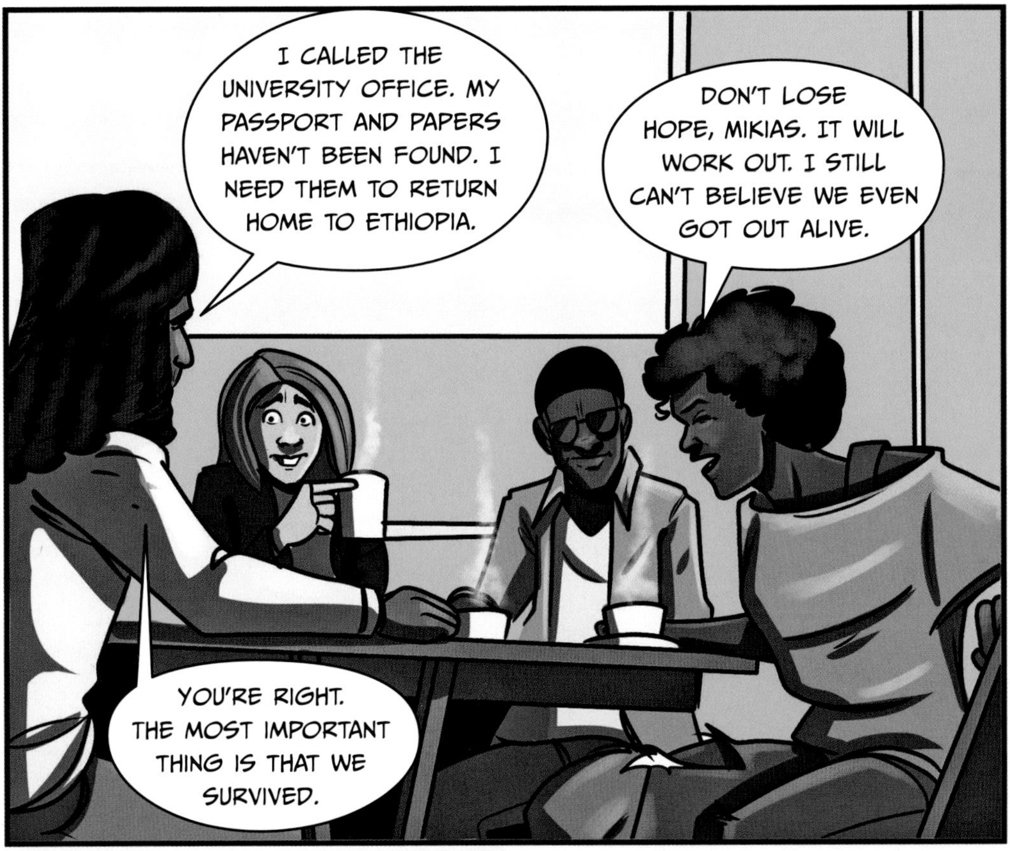
I CALLED THE UNIVERSITY OFFICE. MY PASSPORT AND PAPERS HAVEN'T BEEN FOUND. I NEED THEM TO RETURN HOME TO ETHIOPIA.
DON'T LOSE HOPE, MIKIAS. IT WILL WORK OUT. I STILL CAN'T BELIEVE WE EVEN GOT OUT ALIVE.
YOU'RE RIGHT. THE MOST IMPORTANT THING IS THAT WE SURVIVED.

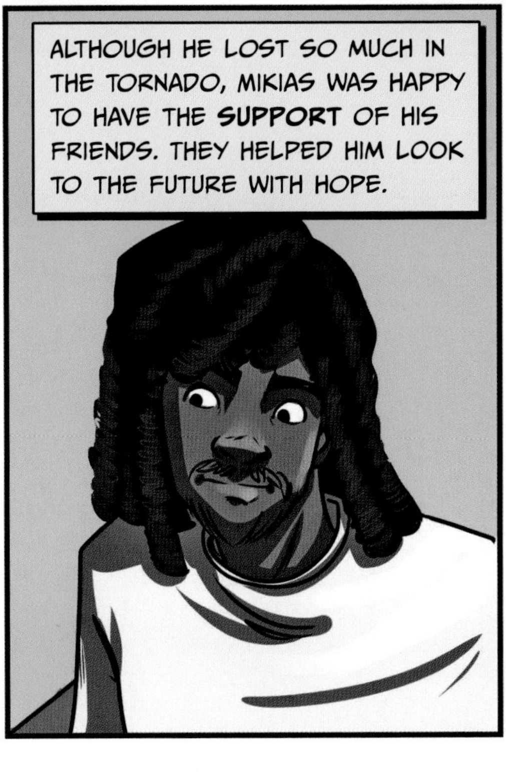
ALTHOUGH HE LOST SO MUCH IN THE TORNADO, MIKIAS WAS HAPPY TO HAVE THE **SUPPORT** OF HIS FRIENDS. THEY HELPED HIM LOOK TO THE FUTURE WITH HOPE.

THE TORNADO AT UNION UNIVERSITY WAS JUST ONE OF 87 TWISTERS THAT HIT SEVERAL STATES OVER A 2-DAY PERIOD. THIS EVENT IS KNOWN AS THE SUPER TUESDAY TORNADO **OUTBREAK**. WHILE NOBODY AT THE UNIVERSITY DIED, OTHERS WERE NOT AS LUCKY. THE TORNADOES KILLED 57 PEOPLE AND INJURED HUNDREDS MORE IN ALABAMA, ARKANSAS, KENTUCKY, AND IN OTHER PARTS OF TENNESSEE.

WHAT IS A TORNADO?

Tornadoes form from violent thunderstorms. When high-speed winds from inside a thunderstorm move over each other, they can form a spinning tube of wind. This tube is positioned sideways above the ground. When the ground is warm, hot air rises above it. This can make the tube of air turn so that it is straight up. A funnel cloud forms if the tube spins fast enough. When it hits the ground, it becomes a tornado.

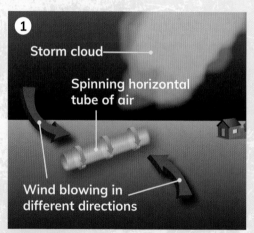

1. Storm cloud — Spinning horizontal tube of air — Wind blowing in different directions

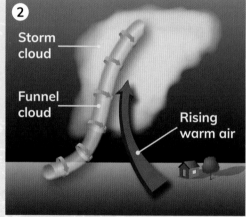

2. Storm cloud — Funnel cloud — Rising warm air

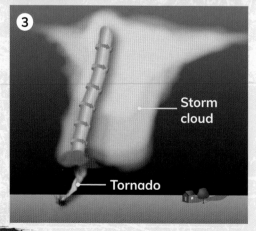

3. Storm cloud — Tornado

A TORNADO CAN ONLY FORM IF THERE IS A LOT OF WARM, RISING AIR. THE TORNADO'S WINDS SLOW DOWN AND STOP WHEN THE SOURCE OF RISING AIR RUNS OUT.

The strength of the wind inside a tornado is measured on the Fujita (foo-JEE-tuh) Scale. An F0 tornado is the weakest and F5 is the strongest. F5 tornadoes have winds faster than 260 miles per hour (418 kph) and can blow a whole house off the ground!

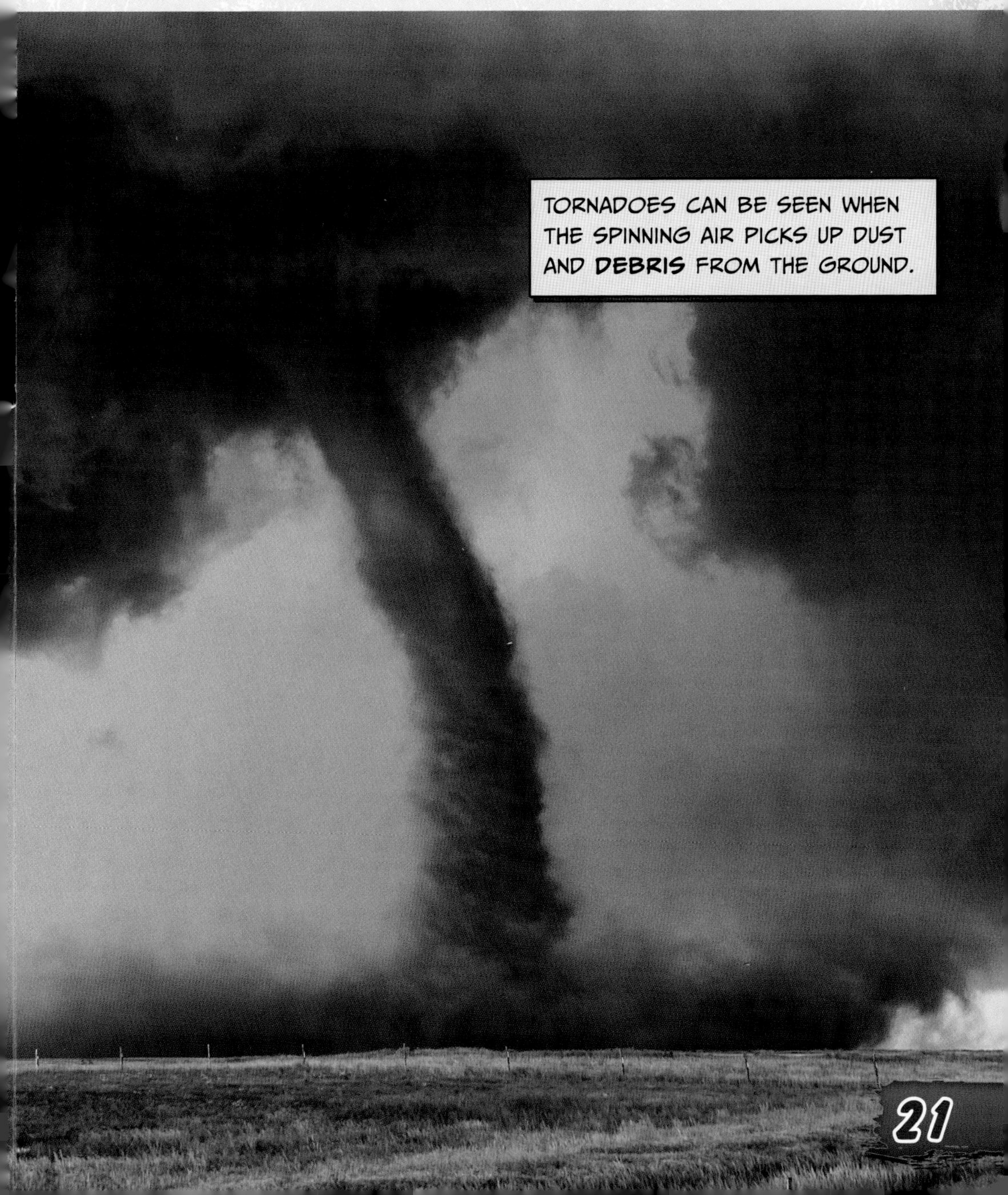
TORNADOES CAN BE SEEN WHEN THE SPINNING AIR PICKS UP DUST AND **DEBRIS** FROM THE GROUND.

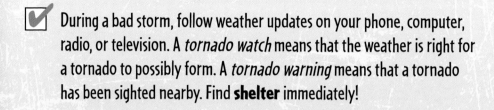

KEEP SAFE

Here are some tornado safety tips.

☑ During a bad storm, follow weather updates on your phone, computer, radio, or television. A *tornado watch* means that the weather is right for a tornado to possibly form. A *tornado warning* means that a tornado has been sighted nearby. Find **shelter** immediately!

☑ Keep in mind that a twister can form suddenly with no warning. Just before a tornado hits, the sky may have a greenish color, there may be **hail**, or there could be a large, dark cloud. Any of these signs means you should rush to take cover.

☑ The safest place to be during a tornado is underground. If you're in a house or other building with no underground shelter, go to the ground floor. Try to find a small space with no windows. Place a mattress or heavy blanket over your head to protect yourself from falling debris.

☑ It is not safe to be in a car during a tornado. Instead, get out and find shelter in a building. If there isn't one nearby, lie in a ditch with your hands over your head. Stay away from trees, which can fall on top of you.

GLOSSARY

debris the broken pieces of something that has been destroyed

dorm short for dormitory room; a room that is used by a college student for studying and sleeping

grateful feeling thankful for something that has been done

hail hard balls of ice that fall from the sky during hailstorms

outbreak a sudden increase in the activity of something

passport a document that shows someone's photo and the country they belong to

protect to keep safe

shelter protection from the outside world and its weather

siren a device that gives off loud warning sounds

support to help and encourage

tornado a violent, whirling column of air that moves over the land and can cause much destruction

twister another, less scientific word for a tornado

INDEX

READ MORE

Murray, Julie. *Tornadoes (Wild Weather)*. Minneapolis: Abdo Zoom (2018).

Rathburn, Betsy. *Tornadoes (Blastoff! Readers. Natural Disasters)*. Minneapolis: Bellwether Media (2020).

Raum, Elizabeth. *Tornadoes! (Natural Disasters)*. Mankato, MN: Amicus (2017).

LEARN MORE ONLINE

1. Go to **www.factsurfer.com**

2. Enter **"Tornado Terror"** into the search box.

3. Click on the cover of this book to see a list of websites.